-eam as in ice cream

Carey Molter

Consulting Editor Monica Marx, M.A./Reading Specialist

Published by SandCastle™, an imprint of ABDO Publishing Company, 4940 Viking Drive, Edina, Minnesota 55435.

Printed in the United States.

Credits
Edited by: Pam Price
Curriculum Coordinator: Nancy Tuminelly
Cover and Interior Design and Production: Mighty Media
Photo Credits: BananaStock Ltd., Brand X Pictures, Corel, Hemera, PhotoDisc, Stockbyte

Library of Congress Cataloging-in-Publication Data

Molter, Carey, 1973-
    -Eam as in ice cream / Carey Molter.
      p. cm. -- (Word families. Set VIII)
    Summary: Introduces, in brief text and illustrations, the use of the letter combination "eam" in such words as "cream," "team," "dream," and "gleam."
    ISBN 1-59197-273-6
    1. Readers (Primary) [1. Vocabulary. 2. Reading.] I. Title.

PE1119 .M594 2003
428.1--dc21
                                          2002038209

SandCastle™ books are created by a professional team of educators, reading specialists, and content developers around five essential components that include phonemic awareness, phonics, vocabulary, text comprehension, and fluency. All books are written, reviewed, and leveled for guided reading, early intervention reading, and Accelerated Reader® programs and designed for use in shared, guided, and independent reading and writing activities to support a balanced approach to literacy instruction.

Let Us Know

After reading the book, SandCastle would like you to tell us your stories about reading. What is your favorite page? Was there something hard that you needed help with? Share the ups and downs of learning to read. We want to hear from you! To get posted on the ABDO Publishing Company Web site, send us e-mail at:

sandcastle@abdopub.com

SandCastle Level: Transitional

-eam Words

cream

scream

seam

steam

stream

team

The cherries are on top
of whipped cream.

The scary movie made
Ken and Dean scream.

The baseball has a red
seam.

Steam makes the train go.

Carl and his dad fish in the stream.

The team wears white
and orange uniforms.

Bob's Dream

There is a cat named Bob.

Bob is on the swim team.

Bob likes to drink warm cream.

He likes his nose to be warmed by the steam.

Then Bob falls asleep
and has a dream.

There is a stream
in his dream.

The stream gleams.

Bob jumps
into the stream.

Bob screams!

The stream is made
of cream!

What a great dream!

Look at Bob beam!
He loves to dream
about cream!

The -eam Word Family

beam	scream
cream	seam
dream	steam
gleam	stream
ream	team

Glossary

Some of the words in this list may have more than one meaning. The meaning listed here reflects the way the word is used in the book.

beam	to have a really big smile
gleam	to shine or glow
seam	the line formed by sewing two pieces of material together
steam	the vapor that is made when water boils
stream	a flow of water such as a brook or small river

About SandCastle™

A professional team of educators, reading specialists, and content developers created the SandCastle™ series to support young readers as they develop reading skills and strategies and increase their general knowledge. The SandCastle™ series has four levels that correspond to early literacy development in young children. The levels are provided to help teachers and parents select the appropriate books for young readers.

Emerging Readers
(no flags)

Beginning Readers
(1 flag)

Transitional Readers
(2 flags)

Fluent Readers
(3 flags)

These levels are meant only as a guide. All levels are subject to change.

To see a complete list of SandCastle™ books and other nonfiction titles from ABDO Publishing Company, visit www.abdopub.com or contact us at:

4940 Viking Drive, Edina, Minnesota 55435 • 1-800-800-1312 • fax: 1-952-831-1632